S0-ADD-115

quick and easy meals for
slimmers

Styling and Food DONNA HAY
Photography WILLIAM MEPPEM

TRIDENT PRESS
INTERNATIONAL

Introduction

There are many books which supply the weight-conscious with kilojoule (calorie) counted recipes and which offer advice on how to lose weight. But there are very few which present the slimmer with complete meals for everyday eating. The recipes in this book are presented as complete main meals which the home cook will find are good enough to feed to the whole family. This book proves that weight loss and healthy eating need not be boring nor does it mean that ethnic foods have to be avoided. The secret is to adapt recipes when necessary or to look for the low-fat options in your favourite cuisines.

Published by:
TRIDENT PRESS INTERNATIONAL
801. 12th Avenue South
Suite 400
Naples, Fl 34102 U.S.A
(c) Trident Press
Tel: (239) 649 7077
Fax: (239) 649 5832
Email: tridentpress@worldnet.att.net
Website: www.trident-international.com

Quick & Easy Meals for Slimmers

Production Manager: Anna Maguire
Food Photography: William Meppem
Food & Styling: Donna Hay.

Recipe Development: Donna Hay

All rights reserved. No part of this book may be stored, reproduced or transmitted in any form or by any means without written permission of the publisher, except in the case of brief quotations embodied in critical articles and reviews.

Includes Index
ISBN 1 582794634
EAN 9 781582 79463 1
UPC 6 15269 94634 3

Second Edition 2003
Printed in Colombia

ABOUT THIS BOOK

NUTRITIONAL ANALYSIS

Each recipe has been computer-analysed for its kilojoule (calorie), fat, fibre and carbohydrate content and have been rated according to the following guidelines:
Fat (grams per serve): less than 5 g – low; 5-10 g – medium; greater than 10 g – high.
Fibre (grams per serve): greater than 4 g – high; 2-4 g – medium; less than 2 g – low.

A NOTE ABOUT MILK

Similar types of milk in different areas may have differing names but milks carry a nutritional information panel which can help you decide the best type to buy.
Skim milk has virtually all fat and cholesterol removed, but retains a full complement of calcium, protein and minerals. It has the least fat and kilojoules (calories) of all milks.
Modified low-fat milks have a fat content similar to skim milk, but with added calcium, protein and lactose. This gives them a richer taste than skim milk.
Modified reduced-fat milks have about half the fat and cholesterol of regular milk, but a creamier taste.
To keep the fat and kilojoule (calorie) content as low as possible, this book uses low-fat milk such as skim or modified low-fat milk. In most cases a modified reduced-fat milk may be substituted but

remember the fat and kilojoule (calorie) content of the recipe will increase.

CANNED FOODS

Can sizes vary between countries and manufacturers. You may find the quantities in this book are slightly different to what is available. Purchase and use the can size nearest to the suggested size in the recipe.

WHAT'S IN A TABLESPOON?

AUSTRALIA
1 tablespoon = 20 mL or 4 teaspoons
NEW ZEALAND
1 tablespoon = 15 mL or 3 teaspoons
UNITED KINGDOM
1 tablespoon = 15 mL or 3 teaspoons
The recipes in this book were tested in Australia where a 20 mL tablespoon is standard. The tablespoon in the New Zealand and the United Kingdom sets of measuring spoons is 15 mL. For recipes using baking powder, gelatine, bicarbonate of soda, small quantities of flour and cornflour, simply add another teaspoon for each tablespoon specified.

Recipes with * indicate that the recipe is included in this book. Those without are included as serving suggestions.

Contents

A Plan for Losing Weight

Remember not all kilojoules
(calories) are equal
1 g fat = 38 kJ/9 Cals
1 g alcohol = 29 kJ/7 Cals
1 g protein = 17 kJ/4 Cals
1 g carbohydrate = 16 kJ/
4 Cals

The sensible slimmer will not only count kilojoules (calories) but will also consider the foods which they choose to eat. Not all kilojoules (calories) are equal, for example 1 gram of fat supplies 38 kilojoules (9 Calories) whereas 1 gram of carbohydrate supplies 16 kilojoules (4 Calories). In addition the body processes foods differently, for example carbohydrate-rich foods require lots of energy for conversion into body fat and stimulate the metabolism just as exercise does. Whereas fatty foods need very little energy for conversion to body fat and slip easily into fat cells. A weight loss plan should aim for a low-fat, high-fibre and high-carbohydrate intake.

Most foods are a combination of protein, fat and carbohydrate with varying amounts of each. For the purposes of classification however, they are defined according to which nutrient they contain most of – fat, protein or carbohydrate.

This guide will help you to design an eating plan to suit your needs and lifestyle.

FREE FOODS

The term free is used as these foods are virtually free of energy and great for filling an empty stomach. They can be eaten in unlimited amounts.

Free foods include the following:
fresh vegetables except for potatoes, legumes and sweet corn
some fruits such as strawberries, passion fruit rhubarb, lemons and limes
lemon, lime, tomato and vegetable juice
no- or low-kilojoule (calorie) beverages such as tea, coffee, water, mineral water and diet soft drinks
seasonings such as herbs and spices
sauces such soy, tomato and Worcestershire vinegar
low-kilojoule (calorie) fruit spreads, jams and chutneys
marmite, vegemite and promite
no-oil salad dressings
low-kilojoule (calorie) jelly

CARBOHYDRATE FOODS

With the exception of milk and yogurt, carbohydrate foods are mainly plant foods. There are two types of carbohydrates –

starches and naturally occurring sugars. Carbohydrates which release energy slowly (starches) tend to be more satisfying and help control the appetite. Those rich in fibre are best and should be chosen first whenever possible. They will also help you to meet your daily fibre requirements.

Include at least two carbohydrate serves at each main meal and if you like to snack include one or two of your carbohydrate serves as a snack. To make the most of the effect of carbohydrates spread them evenly through the day – this ensures an equal spread of energy-giving food. It also keeps your glycogen stores topped up.

As a guide 1 serve of carbohydrate is equal to:
1 slice of bread
$^1/_2$ bread roll
$^1/_2$ small pocket bread
2-4 crackers or crispbreads
2 plain biscuits
30 g/1 oz breakfast cereal
90 g/3 oz cooked rice or pasta
1 medium potato
125 g/4 oz mashed potato
$^1/_2$ cob sweet corn
90 g/3 oz sweet corn kernels
90 g/3 oz cooked baked beans, lentils, chickpeas or red kidney beans
1 apple, banana, peach or orange
20 medium grapes
4 apricots
3 mandarins or plums
220 g/7 oz fresh fruit salad
$^1/_2$ cup/125 mL/4 fl oz fruit juice
1 cup/250 mL/8 fl oz skim, low- or reduced-fat milk
1 cup/200 g/$6^1/_2$ oz low-fat yogurt
$1^1/_2$ scoops/75 g/$2^1/_2$ oz low-fat ice cream
Recommended daily consumption:
Women 8-10 serves   Men 10-12 serves
Note: 1 serve carbohydrate = 15 g

FIBRE

A high-fibre diet is beneficial for those attempting to lose weight as it slows down the emptying of the stomach, making you feel full for a longer period of time. Other important health benefits associated with an adequate soluble dietary fibre intake include lowering blood cholesterol and a better control of blood sugar levels (particularly beneficial for diabetics). The best sources of soluble fibre include: rolled oats, legumes such as dried peas and beans, lentils and fruit.

Additional benefits of fibre associated with the insoluble component include prevention of constipation and some cancers of the bowel and breast. The best sources include: vegetables, nuts, seeds, fruit and grains such as wheat, rice, barley, corn and rye. To ensure a balanced intake of both soluble and insoluble dietary fibre a variety of foods should be consumed each day. To prevent dehydration remember to drink 6-8 glasses (1.5-2 litres) of fluid each day when consuming a diet that includes adequate dietary fibre.
Recommended daily consumption: 25-30 g

PROTEIN
In developed countries protein is generally eaten in larger amounts than the body needs. Eating smaller quantities of protein will help reduce energy and fat intake as well as weight. The body requires only 40 g protein per day – this is the equivalent of 125 g/4 oz lean steak plus 45 g/1^1/2 oz cheese.
As a guide 1 serve of protein is equal to:
30 g/1 oz cooked lean meat such as lamb, beef, pork or veal
30 g/1 oz cooked lean chicken or turkey (skin removed)
45 g/1^1/2 oz fresh or frozen fish
2 thin slices reduced-salt and -fat ham
1 slice smoked salmon
45 g/1^1/2 oz canned salmon, tuna, mackeral or crab in brine or springwater
5 large prawns, clams or scallops
12 raw oysters
3-4 canned sardines
60 g/2 oz low-fat cottage or ricotta cheese
30 g/1 oz reduced-fat Cheddar cheese
1 egg
Recommended daily consumption:
4-5 serves = 100-200 g/3^1/2-6^1/2 oz
Main meal = 3 serves – 90-125 g/3-4 oz
Lunch = 1-2 serves – 30-60 g/1-2 oz

FATS
The less fat you eat the better. All fats are equally fattening but their effect on blood vessel health is different. Monounsaturated and polyunsaturated fats are preferred as they assist in lowering blood fats and therefore the risk of heart and blood vessel disease.

As a guide 1 serve of fat is equal to:
1 teaspoon butter, magarine, oil or tahini paste
^{1}/8 avocado
1 rasher lean bacon
1 tablespoon cream
1 tablespoon cream cheese
1 tablespoon salad dressing
5 small olives
Recommended daily consumption: Not more than four serves (20 g/^{3}/4 oz)

EXERCISE
Exercise should be included in any weight loss or healthy lifestyle plan. A low-fat, high-carbohydrate diet prevents weight and fat gain, while exercise helps with their removal. One of the reasons fat (weight) is regained is because an overly strict food intake drops the body's metabolism and so defeats the purpose of reducing your energy intake to lose weight. However if energy (food) intake is reduced modestly and exercise added then metabolism will not drop.
There are three types of activity which use energy:
1 *Basal (resting) metabolic rate (BMR).* This is the energy used while the body is at rest and it accounts for 70% of energy used. Raising your BMR is important for weight loss and exercise is one of the key factors in raising it.
2 *Thermic effect of exercise.* This is the energy spent when you use your muscles – physical exercise. This is the second largest part of daily energy expenditure and it accounts for 20% of energy use.
3 *Thermic effect of food.* This is the energy used to digest food. As the amount of carbohydrate eaten increases and fat intake decreases, the thermic effect rises, hence the desirability of a low-fat, high-carbohydrate meal plan.

Choose an exercise that you enjoy, that fits into your lifestyle and that you can maintain for 30 minutes or more at one time. One of the easiest and most popular forms of exercise is walking.

Before starting an exercise program have a check up with your doctor and remember if you are not used to exercising don't overdo it at the start.
Minimum recommended weekly exercise:
Three sessions of at least 30 minutes

Flavours of the Orient

In recent times the cuisines of the Orient have become increasingly popular. This is not just because of their wonderful fresh flavours but also because many of the dishes they offer easily fit into our healthier eating patterns. This selection of recipes demonstrates just how easily the slimmer or health-conscious can experience the enticing tastes of the Orient.

Try cooking rice in the microwave to accompany Oriental meals; it does not save time but you are guaranteed a perfect result and there is no messy saucepan at the end of the cooking time. For instructions see hint on page 60.

THAI CHILLI FISH CAKES

260 kilojoules/62 Calories per fish cake – low fibre; low fat; negligible carbohydrate

500 g/1 lb boneless firm
white fish fillets
2 fresh red chillies, chopped
2 stalks fresh lemon grass, finely chopped, or 1 teaspoon dried lemon grass, soaked in hot water until soft
2 tablespoons chopped fresh coriander
1 tablespoon finely grated fresh ginger
2 teaspoons ground cumin
1 teaspoon finely grated lime rind
1 egg white
sweet chilli sauce

1 Place fish, chillies, lemon grass, coriander, ginger, cumin, lime rind and egg white in a food processor and process until smooth.

2 Take 3 tablespoons of mixture and shape into patties.

3 Heat a nonstick frying pan over a medium heat, add fish cakes and cook for 2-3 minutes each side or until golden and cooked through.

Serving suggestion: Serve warm with chilli sauce for dipping.

Makes 8

BAKED MARINATED FISH

851 kilojoules/203 Calories per serve – low fibre; low fat; 1 serve carbohydrate

Oven temperature
180°C, 350°F, Gas 4

4 small whole fish, such as snapper, bream, whiting, sea perch, cod or haddock, cleaned and scaled
8 kaffir lime leaves
8 thin slices lemon

HERBED SPICE MIX
4 spring onions, shredded
2 fresh green chillies, chopped
3 tablespoons shredded fresh basil
2 tablespoons chopped fresh coriander
1 tablespoon cumin seeds
4 tablespoons mango chutney
2 tablespoons reduced-salt soy sauce

1 Rinse fish under cold water and pat dry with absorbent kitchen paper. Place 2 lime leaves and 2 lemon slices in the cavity of each fish and place in a baking dish lined with nonstick baking paper.

2 To make spice mix, place spring onions, chillies, basil, coriander, cumin seeds, chutney and soy sauce in a bowl and mix to combine.

3 Spread spice mix over both sides of fish and bake for 30 minutes or until flesh flakes when tested with a fork.

Serves 4

For an authentic flavour use Thai basil if available.

Previous page: Steamed Chinese Greens, Baked Marinated Fish, Steamed Jasmine Rice
Right: Thai Chilli Fish Cakes

STEAMED CHINESE GREENS

522 kilojoules/124 Calories per serve – high fibre; low fat; 1 serve carbohydrate

315 g/10 oz Chinese broccoli
(gai lum), chopped
250 g/8 oz bok choy (Chinese
leaves), chopped
155 g/5 oz snake (yard-long) or
green beans, chopped
2 tablespoons shredded fresh ginger
^{1}/3 cup/90 mL/3 fl oz oyster sauce
1 tablespoon honey
2 teaspoons sesame seeds

1   Place broccoli (gai lum), bok choy
(Chinese leaves) and beans in a steamer
over boiling water and steam until
vegetables are bright green and tender.

2   Place ginger, oyster sauce and honey
in a saucepan over a medium heat,
bring to simmering and simmer for
1 minute. To serve, place greens on a
serving plate, spoon over sauce and
scatter with sesame seeds.

Serves 4

Chinese broccoli (gai lum) is
a popular Asian vegetable.
It has dark green leaves on
firm stalks often with small
white flowers. The leaves,
stalks and flowers are all
used in cooking. To prepare,
remove leaves from stalks
and peel, then chop both
leaves and stalks and use as
directed in the recipe.

HONEY SESAME CHICKEN

1009 kilojoules/240 Calories per serve – low fibre; medium fat; 1 serve carbohydrate

1 teaspoon sesame oil
2 onions, chopped
2 teaspoons finely grated fresh ginger
2 boneless chicken breast fillets, chopped
1 tablespoon sesame seeds
4 tablespoons salt-reduced soy sauce
2 tablespoons honey

1 Heat oil in a nonstick frying pan or wok over a high heat, add onions and ginger and stir-fry for 4 minutes or until onions are soft.

2 Add chicken and stir-fry until brown. Add sesame seeds, soy sauce and honey and stir-fry for 4 minutes longer or until chicken is tender.

Serves 4

For a refreshing and healthy finish to an Oriental meal serve a platter of chilled seasonal fresh fruit.

VEGETABLE SOY NOODLES

1437 kilojoules/342 Calories per serve – high fibre; low fat; 4 serves carbohydrate

315 g/10 oz hokkien noodles
6 shallots, chopped
1 clove garlic, crushed
185 g/6 oz broccoli, chopped
125 g/4 oz snow peas (mangetout)
1 red pepper, chopped
$1/3$ cup/90 mL/3 fl oz dry white wine
3 tablespoons kechap manis
2 tablespoons hoisin sauce

1 Place noodles in a bowl, pour over hot water to cover then using a fork pull noodles apart. Stand for 5 minutes, then drain and set aside.

2 Heat a nonstick frying pan or wok over a high heat, add shallots and garlic and stir-fry for 2 minutes. Add broccoli, snow peas (mangetout), red pepper, wine, kechap manis and hoisin sauce and stir-fry for 3 minutes. Add noodles and cook for 2 minutes or until noodles are soft and vegetables are tender crisp. Serve immediately.

Serves 4

Hokkien noodles are one type of fresh egg noodle and are avaiable from Oriental food stores and some supermarkets. Some noodles contain added oil, so check the label for fat content when purchasing and choose the brand with the least.

*Vegetable Soy Noodles,
Honey Sesame Chicken*

EASY VIETNAMESE
*Rice Paper Rolls
*Warm Pork and
Mint Salad
Steamed Rice
*Chilled Nashis with Lime
(see hint this page)

RICE PAPER ROLLS

94 kilojoules/22 Calories per roll – low fibre; nil fat; 0.3 serve carbohydrate

12 Oriental rice papers rounds

VEGETABLE FILLING
60 g/2 oz shredded carrot
60 g/2 oz shredded snow peas
(mangetout)
30 g/1 oz bean sprouts
3 tablespoons fresh mint leaves
3 tablespoons fresh basil leaves
3 tablespoons fresh coriander leaves
sweet chilli sauce

1   Dip a rice paper round into warm water, then place on a clean teatowel to absorb excess moisture.

2   To assemble, place a little of the carrot, snow peas (mangetout), bean sprouts, mint, basil and coriander along the centre of rice paper round leaving a 2 cm/³/4 in border.

3   To roll, fold up one edge of rice paper over filling to form base of roll, then roll up to enclose filling. Repeat with remaining rice paper rounds and filling to make 12 rolls.

Serving suggestion: Serve immediately with chilli sauce for dipping.

Makes 12 rolls

Oriental rice paper is made from a paste of ground rice and water which is stamped into rounds and dried. When moistened the brittle sheets become flexible. Sold in sealed packets rice paper can be purchased from Oriental food stores.

WARM PORK AND MINT SALAD

769 kilojoules/183 Calories per serve – medium fibre; low fat; 0.5 serve carbohydrate

6 shallots, chopped
2 tablespoons shredded fresh ginger
1 fresh red chilli, chopped
500 g/1 lb lean minced pork
3 tablespoons shredded Vietnamese mint
1 tablespoon brown sugar
¹/4 cup/60 mL/2 fl oz reduced-salt
soy sauce
2 tablespoons lime juice
2 teaspoons Thai fish sauce
250 g/8 oz assorted lettuce leaves
1 cucumber, sliced
60 g/2 oz snow pea (mangetout)
sprouts or watercress

1   Heat a nonstick frying pan or wok over a medium heat, add shallots, ginger and chilli and cook, stirring, for 3 minutes.

2   Add pork and stir-fry for 3-4 minutes or until brown. Stir in mint, sugar, soy sauce, lime juice and fish sauce and stir-fry for 4 minutes or until pork is cooked.

3   Arrange lettuce leaves, cucumber and snow pea (mangetout) sprouts or watercress on a serving platter, top with pork mixture and serve immediately.

Serves 4

For an easy dessert, serve Chilled Nashis with Lime – cut chilled nashis into thin slices, sprinkle with fresh lime juice and toss. Nashis are at their best during the winter months and this easy dessert is a refreshing and healthy way to end any meal.

If Vietnamese mint is unavailable use ordinary mint instead.

*Clockwise from back: Warm Pork and Mint Salad,
Steamed Rice, Rice Paper Rolls,
Chilled Nashis with Lime*

Salad Meals

No longer should salads be throught of as rabbit or boring diet food. As these recipes show modern salads are a complex mix of fresh foods which are designed to be enjoyed by anyone who loves good food. Just remember to choose a no- or low-oil dressing and go easy on ingredients such as cheese, bacon, ham and anything preserved in oil. Use this selection of innovative salads to give you ideas for your own creations.

VEGETARIAN CHOICE
*Roasted Vegetable Salad
*Soda Bread
*Herbed Yogurt Spread

HERBED YOGURT SPREAD

42 kilojoules/10 Calories per tablespoon – nil fibre; low fat; negligible carbohydrate

2 tablespoons chopped fresh basil
1 tablespoon snipped fresh chives
1 clove garlic, chopped
1 cup/200 g/6^1/$_2$ oz low-fat natural yogurt
1 tablespoon lemon juice
freshly ground black pepper

Place basil, chives, garlic, yogurt, lemon juice and black pepper to taste in a food processor or blender and process to combine.

Makes 1 cup/250 mL/8 fl oz

SODA BREAD

678 kilojoules/161 Calories per slice – low fibre; low fat; 1.8 serves carbohydrate

Oven temperature
200°C, 400°F, Gas 4

4 cups/500 g/1 lb flour
60 g/2 oz butter, softened
2 teaspoons bicarbonate of soda
1 teaspoon chilli powder
1^1/$_4$ cups/315 mL/ 10 fl oz buttermilk

1   Place flour, butter, bicarbonate of soda, chilli powder and milk in a food processor and process to make a soft dough.

2   Turn dough onto a lightly floured surface and knead briefly. Divide dough into half and shape each portion into a loaf. Place dough in two small 8 x 26 cm/ 3^1/$_4$ x 10^1/$_2$ in nonstick loaf tins and bake for 25 minutes or until loaves sound hollow when tapped on the base. Turn onto wire racks to cool. Serve warm with Herbed Yogurt Spread.

The nutritional analysis is based on each loaf cutting into eight slices.
Freeze the second loaf to have on hand as an accompaniment to a salad meal in the future.

Makes 2 loaves

ROASTED VEGETABLE SALAD

1002 kilojoules/239 Calories per serve – high fibre; medium fat; 2 serves carbohydrate

Oven temperature
180°C, 350°F, Gas 4

3 bulbs fennel, cut into wedges
2 sweet potatoes, peeled and chopped
12 shallots, peeled
olive oil spray
1 teaspoon cumin seeds
315 g/10 oz green beans, blanched
185 g/6 oz rocket leaves
155 g/5 oz reduced-fat feta cheese, chopped
2-3 tablespoons balsamic vinegar
freshly ground black pepper

1   Place fennel, sweet potatoes and shallots in a nonstick baking dish and spray with olive oil. Sprinkle with cumin seeds and bake for 30-35 minutes or until vegetables are soft and golden. Set aside to cool for 10-15 minutes or until vegetables are warm.

2   Place vegetables in a serving bowl, add beans, rocket, cheese, vinegar and black pepper to taste and toss.

The shallots used in this recipe are the French échalote. If unavailable red or yellow shallots used in Asian cooking or pickling onions can be used instead.

Serves 4

THAI SQUID SALAD

832 kilojoules/198 Calories per serve – high fibre; low fat; 1 serve carbohydrate

3 squid (calamari) tubes, cleaned
185 g/6 oz green beans, sliced lengthwise
2 tomatoes, cut into wedges
1 small green pawpaw, peeled,
seeded and shredded
4 spring onions, sliced
30 g/1 oz fresh mint leaves
30 g/1 oz fresh coriander leaves
1 fresh red chilli, chopped

LIME DRESSING
2 teaspoons brown sugar
3 tablespoons lime juice
1 tablespoon fish sauce

1 Using a sharp knife, make a single cut down the length of each squid (calamari) tube and open out. Cut parallel lines down the length of the squid (calamari), taking care not to cut right the way through the flesh. Make more cuts in the opposite direction to form a diamond pattern.

2 Heat a nonstick char-grill or frying pan over a high heat, add squid (calamari) and cook for 1-2 minutes each side or until tender. Remove from pan and cut into thin strips.

3 Place squid (calamari), beans, tomatoes, pawpaw, spring onions, mint, coriander and chilli in a serving bowl.

4 To make dressing, place sugar, lime juice and fish sauce in a screwtop jar and shake well. Drizzle over salad and toss to combine. Cover and stand for 20 minutes before serving.

Serving suggestion: Soy Rice Noodles – boil 375 g/12 oz fresh rice noodles, drain and sprinkle with a little reduced-salt soy sauce. Scatter with a few toasted sesame seeds and toss to combine.

Serves 4

THAI SALAD MEAL
*Thai Squid Salad
*Soy Rice Noodles
(see serving suggestion)
Fresh Fruit with
Lemon Sorbet (choose one
of the many low-kilojoule
(calorie) sorbets available
from supermarkets)

Previous pages: Soda Bread, Herbed Yogurt Spread, Roasted Vegetable Salad
Right: Thai Squid Salad, Soy Rice Noodles

ITALIAN CHICKEN SALAD

1140 kilojoules/271 Calories per serve – medium fibre; medium fat; 0.6 serve carbohydrate

3 boneless chicken breast fillets, all
visible fat and skin removed
olive oil spray
125 g/4 oz baby English spinach leaves
125 g/4 oz green beans, blanched
1 red onion, thinly sliced
2 tablespoons small capers, drained

VINEGAR AND PRUNE DRESSING
8 pitted prunes
1 tablespoon fresh oregano leaves
shredded rind of 1 lemon
1 teaspoon sugar
1/2 cup/125 mL/4 fl oz red wine vinegar

1 Heat a nonstick char-grill or frying pan over a high heat. Lightly spray chicken with olive oil, add to pan and cook for 2-3 minutes each side or until tender. Remove from pan and set aside to cool.

2 To make dressing, place prunes, oregano, lemon rind, sugar and vinegar in a saucepan over a low heat, bring to simmering and simmer for 5 minutes.

3 To assemble salad, cut chicken breasts into thin slices. Arrange spinach, beans, onion, chicken and capers attractively on serving plates. Drizzle a little warm dressing over the salad and serve immediately. Serve any remaining dressing separately.

Serves 4

For the slimmers and the health-conscious a nonstick frying pan is essential. Nonstick cookware means that you can avoid using added fat or as in this recipe only a very small quantity is required.

WARM POTATO SALAD

372 kilojoules/89 Calories per serve – medium fibre; low fat; 1.5 serves carbohydrate

500 g/1 lb baby new potatoes

MUSTARD DRESSING
2 tablespoons wholegrain mustard
2 tablespoons chopped fresh parsley
2 teaspoons chopped capers
1 clove garlic, crushed
1 tablespoon lemon juice
freshly ground black pepper

1 Cook potatoes in boiling water until just tender. Drain well and place in a heatproof bowl.

2 To make dressing, place mustard, parsley, capers, garlic, lemon juice and black pepper to taste in a bowl and mix to combine. Spoon dressing over hot potatoes and toss to combine. Serve immediately.

Serves 4

Iced water or mineral water makes a refreshing and non-calorific drink to serve with meals. For added appeal serve with a slice of lemon, lime or orange.

Italian Chicken Salad, Warm Potato Salad

Pasta, Pasta, Pasta

Once thought of as fattening and therefore a food that should be avoided by slimmers, it is now realised that pasta is a high-carbohydrate, low-fat food which is ideal for those wanting to lose weight. These recipes present the cook with imaginative and healthy ways to use this wonderful food. Avoid the creamy high-fat pasta sauces and excessive amounts of cheese and you can't go wrong.

MARINATED TOMATO SALAD

464 kilojoules/110 Calories per serve – low fibre; low fat; 0.5 serve carbohydrate

4 tomatoes, thickly sliced
125 g/4 oz reduced-fat feta
cheese, chopped
$^1/_2$ red onion, sliced
3 tablespoons fresh basil leaves

BALSAMIC DRESSING
1 tablespoon brown sugar
$^1/_4$ cup/60 mL/2 fl oz balsamic vinegar
freshly ground black pepper

1 Place tomatoes, cheese, onion and basil in a bowl and toss to combine.

2 To make dressing, place sugar, vinegar and black pepper to taste in a screwtop jar and shake well to combine. Pour dressing over tomato mixture and toss to combine. Cover and marinate, at room temperature, for 20 minutes before serving.

Serves 4

PENNE WITH PEPPER SAUCE

2036 kilojoules/485 Calories per serve – high fibre; low fat; 6 serves carbohydrate

500 g/1 lb penne
fresh Parmesan cheese (optional)

CHAR-GRILLED PEPPER SAUCE
4 red peppers, seeded and halved
1 cup/250 mL/8 fl oz vegetable stock
185 g/6 oz baby English spinach leaves
125 g/4 oz button mushrooms, sliced
2 zucchini (courgettes), thinly sliced
2 tablespoons tomato paste (purée)

1 To make sauce, place peppers, skin side up, under a hot grill and cook for 5-10 minutes or until skins are blistered and charred. Place peppers in a plastic food or paper bag and set aside until cool enough to handle. Remove skins from peppers and chop flesh. Place pepper flesh in a food processor or blender and with machine running, slowly add stock and process until smooth.

2 Transfer pepper mixture to a saucepan, add spinach, mushrooms, zucchini (courgettes) and tomato paste (purée) and mix to combine. Place over a medium heat, bring to simmering and simmer, stirring occasionally, for 5 minutes or until spinach wilts and mushrooms are tender.

3 Cook penne in boiling water in a large saucepan following packet directions. Drain well, place in serving bowls, spoon over hot sauce and top with Parmesan cheese shavings, if using. Serve immediately.

Serves 4

Always cook pasta in plenty of boiling water, the general rule is 4 cups/1 litre/1$^3/_4$ pt water to every 125 g/4 oz pasta.

Previous pages: Penne with Pepper Sauce, Marinated Tomato Salad
Right: Apple and Ricotta Strudel

APPLE AND RICOTTA STRUDEL

954 kilojoules/227 Calories per serve – low fibre; medium fat; 2.5 serves carbohydrate

8 sheets filo pastry
vegetable oil spray

RICOTTA AND APPLE FILLING
440 g/14 oz canned unsweetened
pie apples, drained
2 tablespoons brown sugar
90 g/3 oz sultanas
1 cup/250 g/8 oz low-fat ricotta
cheese, drained
2 tablespoons sugar
2 teaspoons cornflour
1 teaspoon ground cinnamon
1 egg white

1 Spray each sheet of pastry lightly with oil, then layer.

2 To make filling, place apples, brown sugar and sultanas in a bowl and mix to combine. Place apple mixture down centre of pastry. Place ricotta cheese, sugar, cornflour, cinnamon and egg white in a bowl and mix to combine. Spoon ricotta mixture over apples.

3 Fold short ends of pastry over filling, then roll to completely enclose. Place strudel on a baking tray lined with nonstick baking paper and bake for 25 minutes or until pastry is crisp and golden.

Serves 6

Oven temperature
180°C, 350°F, Gas 4

For those who love pastry try using filo pastry instead of puff pastry for pies and, as in this recipe, lightly spray the pastry with oil rather than brushing it with oil.

EASY WINTER MEAL
*Spicy Lamb and
Pasta Bake
*Spinach Tabbouleh
*Brownie Cupcakes
(page 68)

SPINACH TABBOULEH

408 kilojoules/97 Calories per serve – high fibre; low fat; 1 serve carbohydrate

1/2 cup/90 g/3 oz burghul
(cracked wheat)
1/2 cup/125 mL/4 fl oz hot water
1/2 bunch/250 g/8 oz English spinach,
leaves shredded
2 tomatoes, chopped
1/2 red onion, chopped
6 tablespoons chopped fresh
flat leaf parsley
4 tablespoons chopped fresh mint
1/3 cup/90 mL/3 fl oz lemon juice
freshly ground black pepper

1 Place burghul (cracked wheat) in a
bowl, pour over water and stand for
10 minutes or until water is absorbed.

2 Add spinach, tomatoes, onion,
parsley, mint, lemon juice and black
pepper to taste and toss to combine.

Serves 4

SPICY LAMB AND PASTA BAKE

1774 kilojoules/422 Calories per serve – high fibre; medium fat; 3 serves carbohydrate

Oven temperature
180°C, 350°F, Gas 4

1 onion, chopped
2 cloves garlic, crushed
1 teaspoon ground cumin
500 g/1 lb lean minced lamb
2 tablespoons chopped fresh mint
2 x 440 g/14 oz canned tomatoes,
undrained and mashed
1/2 cup/125 mL/4 fl oz beef stock
2 eggplant (aubergines), sliced
12 sheets instant (no precooking
required) lasagne

RICOTTA TOPPING
155 g/5 oz low-fat ricotta cheese,
drained
2 tablespoons chopped fresh marjoram
or oregano
freshly ground black pepper

1 Place onion, garlic and cumin in a
nonstick frying pan over a high heat
and cook, stirring, for 5 minutes or
until onion is golden.

2 Add lamb and cook, stirring, for
5 minutes or until meat is brown.
Add mint, tomatoes and stock, bring
to simmering and simmer, stirring
occasionally, for 10 minutes.

3 Layer eggplant (aubergines), lamb
mixture and lasagne sheets in a lightly
greased ovenproof dish, finishing with a
layer of eggplant (aubergines).

4 To make topping, place ricotta
cheese, marjoram or oregano and black
pepper to taste in bowl and mix to
combine. Spread topping over eggplant
(aubergines) and bake for 30 minutes or
until eggplant (aubergines) and pasta
are tender and top is golden.

Serves 4

When using instant (no
precooking required)
lasagne the cooked dish
tends to be moister and the
pasta more tender if the
lasagne sheets are dipped
in warm water before
assembling the dish.

*Spinach Tabbouleh,
Spicy Lamb and Pasta Bake*

CASUAL SPRING MEAL
*Tomato Bruschetta
*Tuna and Lemon Pasta
Tossed Green Salad
(see Easy Salads this page)
Strawberries tossed with
Orange-flavoured Liqueur
or Fresh Orange Juice

Remember exercise is an important part of a healthy lifestyle. It not only helps you lose and maintain a weight it also gives you more energy, lowers blood pressure, improves circulation, reduces blood fats (cholesterol and triglycerides), relieves stress and tension, improves digestion, helps prevent constipation and makes your bones stronger. Walking is one of the easiest and most enjoyable forms of exercise, as it only requires a good pair of walking shoes and nearly everyone can do it.

TOMATO BRUSCHETTA

936 kilojoules/223 Calories per serve – medium fibre; low fat; 3 serves carbohydrate

12 slices crusty Italian bread
2 tomatoes, finely chopped
3 tablespoons small fresh basil leaves
4-6 olives, chopped
1 tablespoon capers, drained
1 tablespoon balsamic vinegar
freshly ground black pepper

1   Place bread under a preheated grill and toast on both sides until golden.

2   Place tomatoes, basil, olives, capers, vinegar and black pepper to taste in a bowl and toss to combine. Just prior to serving, top each toast slice with some of the tomato mixture.

Serves 4

TUNA AND LEMON PASTA

2733 kilojoules/651 Calories per serve – high fibre; medium fat; 6 serves carbohydrate

500 g/1 lb fettuccine
440 g/14 oz canned tuna in spring water, drained and flaked
185 g/6 oz rocket leaves, roughly chopped
155 g/5 oz reduced-fat feta cheese, chopped
1 tablespoon chopped fresh dill
1/4 cup/60 mL/2 fl oz lemon juice
freshly ground black pepper

Cook fettuccine in boiling water in a large saucepan following packet directions. Drain and return pasta to saucepan. Place pan over a low heat, add tuna, rocket, cheese, dill, lemon juice and black pepper to taste and toss to combine. Serve immediately.

Serves 4

EASY SALADS

Many salads do not require a recipe if you have a few basic ingredients and an interesting dressing. Just remember to keep the kilojoules (calories) low by choosing a low- or no-fat dressing. There are a variety of commercial low-fat dressings available or make your own. **Coleslaw** is easily made by shredding cabbage and combining it with grated carrot, diced red or green pepper, diced celery and chopped fresh herbs, then tossing with a dressing of low-fat natural yogurt, wholegrain mustard and freshly ground black pepper.
Tossed green salads are easy to make if you keep 2-3 different types of lettuce and a few fresh herbs, on hand. To make the salad, take a few leaves from each lettuce, wash and dry, tear into pieces and place in a salad bowl, add chopped fresh herbs and black pepper and toss with a little balsamic, sherry or fruit-flavoured vinegar.
Potato salad. When cooking the evening meal, cook extra potatoes, cool then store in the refrigerator. Make the salad by cutting the potatoes in pieces then tossing with a dressing of low-fat natural yogurt, chopped fresh herbs and freshly ground black pepper.

*Tuna and Lemon Pasta,
Tomato Bruschetta*

Hot & Spicy

Here the slimmer will find complete Indian, Mexican and Cajun meals that are sure to be popular with the whole family. For those who are not on a weight reduction program additional carbohydrates such as bread, rice, pasta, noodles or potatoes are the ideal way to bulk up the meal, but still keep it healthy.

SPICY POTATO STEW

588 kilojoules/140 Calories per serve – high fibre; low fat; 1.5 serves carbohydrate

1 onion, finely chopped
2-3 dried red chillies, crushed
2 cloves garlic, chopped
1 teaspoon ground turmeric
2 teaspoons ground cumin
4 small potatoes, quartered
4 baby eggplant (aubergines), halved lengthwise
315 g/10 oz okra, trimmed
4 cups/1 litre/1³/₄ pt vegetable stock
2 tablespoons chopped fresh mint
2 tablespoons chopped fresh coriander
2 teaspoons garam marsala
1 tablespoon lemon juice

1   Place onion, chillies, garlic, turmeric and cumin in a nonstick frying pan over a medium heat and cook for 4 minutes or until onion is soft.

2   Add potatoes, eggplant (aubergines), okra and stock to pan, cover and bring to simmering. Simmer, stirring occasionally, for 25 minutes or until vegetables are soft.

3   Stir in mint, coriander, garam marsala and lemon juice and cook for 3 minutes.

Serves 4

FRAGRANT LENTILS

720 kilojoules/171 Calories per serve – high fibre; low fat; 1.5 serves carbohydrate

1 tablespoon finely grated fresh ginger
1 clove garlic, crushed
1 teaspoon cumin seeds
250 g/8 oz red lentils
3 cups/750 mL/1¹/₄ pt vegetable stock
2 tablespoons lemon juice

Place ginger, garlic and cumin seeds in a saucepan over a medium heat and cook for 1 minute. Stir in lentils, stock and lemon juice, bring to simmering and simmer for 10-15 minutes or until lentils are soft.

Serves 4

Lentils are a good source of vegetable protein, complex carbohydrate and fibre in addition to which they are virtually fat free. They also supply B vitamins, potassium, phosphorus and iron.

SPICY BEANS IN YOGURT

334 kilojoules/80 Calories per serve – medium fibre; low fat; 0.6 serve carbohydrate

1 onion, chopped
1 fresh green chilli, chopped
1 tablespoon black mustard seeds
2 teaspoons cumin seeds
375 g/12 oz green beans, trimmed
1¹/₂ cups/300 g/9¹/₂ oz low-fat natural yogurt
1 tablespoon cornflour blended with ¹/₃ cup/90 mL/3 fl oz water

1   Place onion, chilli and mustard and cumin seeds in nonstick frying pan over a medium heat and cook for 3 minutes or until onion is soft.

2   Add beans and cook, stirring, for 4 minutes or until they change colour. Reduce heat to low. Whisk together yogurt and cornflour mixture, stir into bean mixture and simmer for 5 minutes.

Serves 4

*Previous pages: Spicy Beans in Yogurt, Spicy Potato Stew, Fragrant Lentils
Right: Pappadums, Fresh Onion Relish, Peach Chutney, Tomato and Mint Raita*

Pappadums

98 kilojoules/23 Calories per pappadum – low fibre; low fat; negligible carbohydrate

12 pappadums

Place pappadums under a preheated hot grill and cook until puffed and crisp. Watch the pappadums carefully as they cook very quickly and can burn.

Alternatively, place pappadums in a single layer on absorbent kitchen paper and cook in the microwave on HIGH (100%) for 1-2 minutes or until puffed and crisp.

Makes 12

If your problem is eating too much too quickly, try using chopsticks to eat all your meals. It's a sure way to slow down your eating and might be just the trick you need to eat less.

Tomato and Mint Raita

51 kilojoules/12 Calories per tablespoon – low fibre; low fat; negligible carbohydrate

These dips and relishes can also be served with a range of Indian breads such as roti, naan and chapatti.

2 tomatoes, peeled, seeded and diced
2 tablespoons chopped fresh mint
1 clove garlic, crushed
1 cup/200 g/6^1/2 oz low-fat natural yogurt
1 tablespoon lemon juice
freshly ground black pepper

Place tomatoes, mint, garlic, yogurt, lemon juice and black pepper in a bowl and mix to combine.

Makes 1 cup/250 g/8 oz

Fresh Onion Relish

22 kilojoules/5 Calories per tablespoon – low fibre; low fat; negligible carbohydrate

Low-fat yogurt is low in fat but not necessarily low in sugar. Diet yogurt is low in fat, artificially sweetened and has the least kilojoules (calories). Yogurt is a good source of calcium and phosphorus.

2 onions, finely diced
2 tablespoons chopped fresh parsley
1 teaspoon paprika
pinch cayenne pepper
2 tablespoons lemon juice
sea salt

Place onions, parsley, paprika, cayenne pepper, lemon juice and a little sea salt in a bowl and mix to combine. Cover and refrigerate for at least 1 hour before serving.

Makes 1 cup/250 mL/8 fl oz

Peach Chutney

137 kilojoules/33 Calories per tablespoon – low fibre; low fat; 0.5 serve carbohydrate

To sterilise jars, wash well in hot soapy water, then rinse in hot water and dry for about 30 minutes in an oven set at the lowest possible heat. Ensure jars are completely dry before filling or the preserve will spoil.

2 green apples, peeled and diced
2 peaches, peeled and chopped
^{1}/3 cup/60 g/2 oz brown sugar
60 g/2 oz raisins
1 tablespoon finely grated fresh ginger
1 clove garlic, crushed
^{1}/2 cup/125 mL/4 fl oz white vinegar

Place apples, peaches, sugar, raisins, ginger, garlic and vinegar in a saucepan over a medium heat and bring to the boil. Reduce heat and simmer for 25 minutes or until chutney is thick. Pour into hot sterilised jars. Cover and seal when cold.

Makes 1^1/2 cups/375 mL/12 fl oz

Beef Tortillas with Salsa

BEEF TORTILLAS WITH SALSA

1612 kilojoules/384 Calories per serve – high fibre; medium fat; 3 serves carbohydrate

EASY MEXCIAN
*Beef Tortillas with Salsa
Selection of Fresh Fruit

500 g/1 lb beef eye fillet, trimmed
2 tablespoons chopped fresh oregano
1 clove garlic, crushed
1 teaspoon ground cumin
1 teaspoon chilli powder
1 tablespoon lime juice
8-12 flour tortillas
220 g/7 oz assorted lettuce leaves
1 cup/200 g/6$\frac{1}{2}$ oz low-fat natural
yogurt

CHILLI SALSA
4 tomatoes, peeled, seeded and chopped
1 red onion, chopped
2 fresh red chillies, seeded and chopped
2 tablespoons fresh coriander leaves
1 teaspoon sugar
1 tablespoon lime juice
freshly ground black pepper

Serves 4

1 Place beef in a shallow glass or ceramic dish. Combine oregano, garlic, cumin, chilli powder and lime juice, then rub over beef and marinate for 20 minutes.

2 To make salsa, place tomatoes, onion, chillies, coriander, sugar, lime juice and black pepper to taste in a bowl and mix to combine. Cover and refrigerate until required.

3 Preheat a barbecue to a high heat. Place beef on a lightly oiled barbecue grill and cook for 4 minutes each side or until cooked to your liking.

4 Heat a nonstick frying pan over a medium heat, add tortillas and cook for 30 seconds each side to warm. Cut beef into thin slices, place on tortillas, then top with lettuce leaves, yogurt and salsa and roll up.

A char-grill pan (a cast iron pan with ridges) can be used instead of the barbecue if you wish. To use heat the dry pan over a high heat until very hot, lightly brush beef with oil, place in pan and cook until done to your liking.

CAJUN CHICKEN MEAL
*Cajun Chicken with Salsa
*Corn Bread
Low-fat Ice Cream and Fresh Fruit

This recipe is also good cooked on the barbecue – cook the vegetables on a lightly oiled grill and the chicken on the preheated barbecue plate (griddle).

CAJUN CHICKEN WITH SALSA

1354 kilojoules/322 Calories per serve – medium fibre; medium fat; 1 serve carbohydrate

3 chicken breast fillets, trimmed
2 limes, cut into wedges

CAJUN SPICE MIX
1 tablespoon sweet paprika
1 teaspoon onion powder
1 teaspoon ground cumin
1 teaspoon ground oregano
1 teaspoon ground thyme
$^{1}/_{2}$ teaspoon cayenne pepper

CORN SALSA
3 cobs sweet corn, husks removed
2 red onions, thickly sliced
1 red pepper, cut into thin strips
$^{1}/_{2}$ cup fresh coriander leaves
1 fresh red chilli, chopped
2 tablespoons lime juice
1 tablespoon Worcestershire sauce
freshly ground black pepper

1 To make salsa, cook sweet corn in boiling water for 5-7 minutes or until tender. Drain. Heat a nonstick char-grill pan over a high heat. Add sweet corn, onions and red pepper and cook, turning frequently, until corn is charred and soft and onions and peppers are tender. Remove kernels from sweet corn cobs and place in a bowl. Add onion, red pepper, coriander, chilli, lime juice, Worcestershire sauce and black pepper to taste and mix to combine.

2 To make spice mix, place paprika, onion powder, cumin, oregano, thyme and cayenne pepper in a bowl and mix to combine.

3 Roll chicken in spice mix to coat. Heat a nonstick char-grill or frying pan over a medium heat, add chicken and cook for 2-3 minutes each side or until tender. Cut chicken into thin strips and serve with salsa and lime wedges.

Serves 4

CORN BREAD

647 kilojoules/154 Calories per slice – low fibre; low fat; 2 serves carbohydrate

Oven temperature
220°C, 425°F, Gas 7

The nutritional anaylsis is based on the loaf cutting into 12 slices.
Leftover corn bread is delicious toasted and topped with a little fruit jam for breakfast. It is also a very good source of beta-carotene, B-complex vitamins and iron.

7 g/$^{1}/_{4}$ oz packet dry yeast
$^{1}/_{2}$ teaspoon sugar
1 cup/250 mL/8 fl oz warm water
$2^{1}/_{4}$ cups/280 g/9 oz flour
1 cup/170 g/$5^{1}/_{2}$ oz corn meal (polenta)
2 fresh red chillies, chopped
2 teaspoons ground cumin
2 teaspoons grated lime rind
1 egg

1 Place yeast, sugar and water in a bowl and mix to combine. Set aside in a warm place until frothy.

2 Place flour, corn meal (polenta), chillies, cumin and lime rind in a bowl and mix to combine. Make a well in the centre of the dry ingredients, add egg and yeast mixture and mix to a smooth dough. Knead dough on a lightly floured surface until smooth and elastic, then place in a lightly oiled bowl. Cover and stand in a warm, draught-free place until doubled in size. Punch down and knead for 1 minute.

3 Shape dough into round loaf and place in a 20 cm/8 in nonstick round cake tin. Cover and stand in a warm, draught-free place until doubled in size. Bake for 20-25 minutes or until loaf sounds hollow when tapped on the base.

Makes a 20 cm/8 in round loaf

Cajun Chicken with Salsa, Corn Bread

A Taste of the Mediterranean

Italian food is popular the world over and offers a variety of healthy and tasty dishes for the slimmer. However the cuisine of other countries in this region such as Greece and Spain is becoming increasingly popular and as this chapter shows with a little adaption the foods of these countries can be equally as healthy.

CUCUMBER AND YOGURT DIP

64 kilojoules/15 Calories per 2 tablespoons – low fibre; low fat; negligible carbohydrate

1 small cucumber, peeled, seeded and
chopped
salt
1 tablespoon chopped fresh mint
1 clove garlic, crushed
1¹/₂ cups/300 g/9¹/₂ oz low-fat
natural yogurt
1 tablespoon lemon juice
freshly ground black pepper

1 Place cucumber into a colander, sprinkle with salt and drain for 10 minutes. Rinse under cold running water and place on absorbent kitchen paper to drain.

2 Place cucumber, mint, garlic, yogurt, lemon juice and black pepper to taste in bowl and mix to combine.

Makes 2 cups/500 mL/16 fl oz

UNLEAVENED BREAD

825 kilojoules/196 Calories per round – low fibre; low fat; 2 serves carbohydrate

Oven temperature
220°C, 425°F, Gas 7

4 cups/500 g/1 lb flour
1 teaspoon salt
1 cup/250 mL/8 fl oz water
45g/1¹/₂ oz ghee, melted

1 Combine flour and salt in a bowl and make a well in the centre. Add water and ghee and mix to a smooth dough. Rest dough for 20 minutes.

2 Take 2 tablespoons of dough and roll into balls. Roll each ball to make very thin oval shapes. Place breads on a nonstick baking tray and bake for 2-4 minutes or until lightly golden.

Makes 12 rounds

BEANS IN TOMATO SAUCE

202 kilojoules/48 Calories per serve – high fibre; low fat; 0.5 serve carbohydrate

Zucchini (courgettes),
cauliflower and broccoli
are also delicious cooked
this way.

1 onion, chopped
2 cloves garlic, crushed
440 g/14 oz canned tomatoes,
undrained and mashed
2 tablespoons chopped fresh flat
leaf parsley
1 tablespoon chopped fresh mint
375 g/12 oz green beans, trimmed
freshly ground black pepper

1 Heat a nonstick frying pan over a medium heat, add onion and garlic and cook for 4 minutes or until onion is soft and golden. Stir in tomatoes, parsley and mint, bring to simmering and simmer for 4 minutes.

2 Add beans and cook for 5 minutes or until beans are tender crisp. Season to taste with pepper.

Serves 4

Previous pages: Beans in Tomato
Sauce, Lamb with Quinces
Right: Cucumber and Yogurt Dip,
Unleavened Bread

LAMB WITH QUINCES

803 kilojoules/191 Calories per serve – low fibre; low fat; negligible carbohydrate

500 g/1 lb lamb loin, trimmed
of visible fat
1 onion, chopped
2 quinces, peeled, cored and
cut into thick slices
2 bay leaves
1 cinnamon stick
1 thick strip orange peel
2 cups/500 mL/16 fl oz beef stock
1 cup/250 mL/8 fl oz water
³/4 cup/185 mL/6 fl oz red wine

1   Heat a nonstick frying pan over a
high heat, add lamb and cook for
2 minutes each side or until brown,
remove from pan and set aside.

2   Add onion to pan and cook, stirring,
for 4 minutes or until soft. Add
quinces, bay leaves, cinnamon stick,
orange peel, stock, water and wine,
cover and bring to simmering. Simmer
for 35 minutes or until quinces are
tender. Add extra water if necessary
during cooking.

3   Place lamb on quince mixture and
cook for 5 minutes or until lamb is
heated through. To serve, cut lamb into
thick slices, place on serving plates and
spoon over quince sauce.

Serves 4

Firm pears make a good
alternative to the quinces
in this recipe. However they
do not need to be cooked
as long. If using pears allow
the stock mixture to simmer
for 15 minutes, then add
the pears and cook for
15 minutes longer or until
pears are tender.

SPANISH PAELLA
SUPPER
*Paella
*Tossed Green Salad
with Lemon
(see serving suggestion)
*Orange Salad

PAELLA

2183 kilojoules/520 Calories per serve – high fibre; low fat; 5 serves carbohydrate

2 boneless chicken breast fillets,
skin removed
90 g/3 oz reduced-salt and -fat
ham, sliced
1 onion, chopped
2 cloves garlic, crushed
3 tomatoes, peeled and chopped
1 teaspoon sweet paprika
$^1/_2$ teaspoon saffron threads
4 cups/1 litre/1$^3/_4$ pt chicken stock
350 g/11 oz long grain rice
185 g/6 oz green beans, trimmed
and chopped
1 red pepper, chopped
75 g/2$^1/_2$ oz fresh or frozen peas
4 tablespoons chopped fresh flat
leaf parsley

1   Heat a nonstick frying pan over a high heat, add chicken and cook for 2-3 minutes each side or until tender, remove from pan and set aside to cool. Cut into thin slices.

2   Add ham, onion and garlic to pan and cook, stirring, for 5 minutes or until onion is soft. Add tomatoes, paprika, saffron and stock, cover and bring to the boil.

3   Stir in rice, cover and simmer for 15 minutes or until rice is tender. Add chicken, beans, red pepper, peas and black pepper to taste and simmer for 10 minutes or until vegetables are tender. Scatter with parsley and serve immediately from the pan.

Serving suggestion: Tossed Green Salad with Lemon – place assorted lettuce leaves in a bowl, sprinkle with a little freshly squeezed lemon juice and freshly ground black pepper. Toss and serve immediately.

Serves 4

Paella is a great one-dish meal that is perfect for feeding a crowd. In Spain the paella pan is placed in the centre of the table and the paella is eaten straight from the pan.

ORANGE SALAD

502 kilojoules/120 Calories per serve – medium fibre; low fat; 2 serves carbohydrate

4 oranges
$^1/_4$ cup/60 g/2 oz sugar
1 cinnamon stick
$^3/_4$ cup/185 mL/6 fl oz water
1 teaspoon lemon juice
4 tablespoons reduced-fat
honey-flavoured yogurt

Peel remaining oranges, remove all the white pith, and slice all oranges crossways into 1 cm/$^1/_2$ in thick slices. Place in a heatproof bowl and set aside.

2   Place reserved orange rind, sugar, cinnamon stick, water and lemon juice in saucepan over a medium heat, bring to simmering and simmer for 3 minutes. Remove from heat, cool slightly and pour over oranges. Cover and chill for at least 2 hours or until ready to serve. Serve with yogurt.

When blood oranges are in season they make a spectacular alternative to ordinary oranges in this simple dessert salad. Blood oranges are in season during winter months, however their season is short and they are not always easy to find.

1   Thinly peel the rind from 1 orange. Ensure all the white pith is removed, cut rind into thin strips and set aside.

Serves 4

Paella, Orange Salad

Oven temperature
160°C, 325°F, Gas 3

This low-fat starter makes a great lunch dish when served with a tossed green salad and crusty wholemeal bread or bread rolls.

STUFFED PEPPERS

413 kilojoules/98 Calories per serve – medium fibre; low fat; 0.3 serve carbohydrate

2 small red peppers
2 small yellow or green peppers
2 ripe tomatoes, peeled, quartered and seeds removed
3 tablespoons torn fresh basil leaves
1 clove garlic, thinly sliced
200 g/6¹/₂ oz low-fat ricotta cheese, drained
freshly ground black pepper

1 Cut peppers in half, lengthwise, leaving stem intact. Remove seeds. Place peppers, cut side up, on a nonstick baking tray and bake for 20 minutes.

2 Place tomatoes, basil and garlic in a bowl and mix to combine. Divide tomato mixture between pepper halves, then top with ricotta cheese and black pepper to taste. Increase oven temperature to 200°C/400°F/Gas 6 and bake for 10 minutes or until peppers are tender and filling is hot. To serve, place 1 red pepper and 1 yellow or green pepper half on each serving plate and spoon over some of the pan juices.

Serves 4

BAKED SICILIAN FISH

561 kilojoules/134 Calories per serve – low fibre; low fat; negligible carbohydrate

Oven temperature
200°C, 400°F, Gas 6

Fish is a great food for the slimmer and health-conscious. It is low in kilojoules (calories), fat and cholesterol and is rich in the important Omega-3 fats. Health professionals recommend eating fish at least three times a week – include fresh, frozen and canned for variety and remember to choose low-fat cooking techniques.

4 swordfish, blue eye cod or haddock steaks
1 onion, sliced
3 tablespoons chopped fresh flat leaf parsley
2 tablespoons capers
2 teaspoons finely grated lemon rind
crushed black peppercorns
¹/₂ cup/125 mL/4 fl oz white wine
¹/₂ cup/125 mL/4 fl oz fish stock or water

1 Place fish in a nonstick baking dish and scatter with onion, parsley, capers, lemon rind and black pepper to taste. Combine wine and stock or water and pour over fish.

2 Cover and bake for 10 minutes or until fish flakes when tested with a fork. To serve, place fish on serving plates and spoon over some of the pan juices.

Serving suggestion: Hot Potato Salad – boil or microwave 500 g/1 lb new potatoes until tender, drain and place in bowl. Add 2 tablespoons no-oil mayonnaise, 1 tablespoon chopped fresh dill and ground black pepper to taste and toss to combine.

Serves 4

Stuffed Peppers, Baked Sicilian Fish

Swift & Simple

This selection of menus offers quick and easy ideas for those times when you might be tempted by fast food outlets. Too often it is forgotten just how quickly a nutritious meal can be prepared – the complete meals in this chapter all take less than 30 minutes to prepare and cook, but best of all they use fresh food, taste great and won't ruin your eating plan.

SPEEDY FISH DINNER
*Lime Marinated Fish
*Sweet Potato Mash
*Steamed Greens
with Lime
(see serving suggestion)

LIME MARINATED FISH

671 kilojoules/160 Calories per serve – low fibre; low fat; negligible carbohydrate

**4 thick fish fillets or cutlets
4 kaffir lime leaves, shredded
1 fresh red chilli, chopped
$^1/4$ cup/60 mL/2 fl oz lime juice
1 teaspoon sesame oil**

1   Place fish in a shallow glass or ceramic dish. Scatter with lime leaves and chilli, then sprinkle with lime juice and sesame oil and marinate for 5 minutes.

2   Heat a nonstick char-grill or frying pan over a medium heat. Drain fish, add to pan and cook for 2-4 minutes each side or until flesh flakes when tested with a fork.

Serving Suggestion: Steamed Greens with Lime – steam or microwave 250 g/ 8 oz each of broccoli and asparagus until just tender, drain and place in a serving bowl. Sprinkle with fresh lime juice, add freshly ground black pepper to taste and toss.

Serves 4

If kaffir lime leaves are unavailable use some finely shredded lime rind instead.

SWEET POTATO MASH

734 kilojoules/175 Calories per serve – medium fibre; low fat; 2.5 serves carbohydrate

**750 g/1$^1/2$ lb sweet potatoes, peeled and chopped
1 tablespoon honey
$^1/2$-$^3/4$ cup/125-185 mL/4-6 fl oz
low-fat milk
freshly ground black pepper**

Boil or microwave sweet potatoes until tender. Drain, place in a bowl, add honey, milk and black pepper to taste and mash to a creamy consistency.

Serves 4

Remember exercise requires fuel (kilojoules/calories) which otherwise would be stored as fat. Just 30 minutes of extra walking each day can lead to a 10 kg/22 lb weight loss in a year.

*Previous pages: Lime Marinated Fish, Sweet Potato Mash, Steamed Greens with Lime
Opposite: Vegetarian Turkish Bread, Banana Smoothie*

VEGETARIAN TURKISH BREAD

983 kilojoules/234 Calories per serve – high fibre; medium fat; 1.5 serves carbohydrate

1 cup/250 g/8 oz low-fat ricotta
cheese, drained
2 tablespoons chilli sauce
4 pieces Turkish bread (pide), split
125 g/4 oz baby spinach leaves
1 yellow pepper, chopped
4 olives, chopped
2 tomatoes, sliced
250 g/8 oz asparagus, blanched
lemon wedges

1 Place ricotta cheese and chilli sauce in a bowl and mix to combine. Spread ricotta mixture over half the Turkish bread pieces, then top with spinach, yellow pepper, olives, tomatoes, asparagus and bread tops.

2 Heat a nonstick frying pan over a medium heat, add sandwiches and cook for 4 minutes each side or until golden and heated through. Serve with lemon wedges.

Serving Suggestion: Banana Smoothie – for each smoothie, place 1 banana, 1 cup/250 mL/8 fl oz low-fat milk, 4 tablespoons low-fat natural yogurt, 2 teaspoons honey and 10 ice cubes in a blender and process until frothy.

Serves 4

EASY SANDWICH MEAL
*Vegetarian Turkish Bread
*Banana Smoothie (see serving suggestion)

Turkish bread (pide) is a flat white leavened bread similar to Italian flatbread.
It is usually baked in ovals measuring 30-40 cm/12-16 in.
If Turkish bread (pide) is unavailable country-style Italian bread, rye bread, sour dough, ciabatta or focaccia are all equally good for this sandwich meal.

SEAFOOD MINESTRONE

1800 kilojoules/429 Calories per serve – high fibre; medium fat; 3 serves carbohydrate

1 teaspoon olive oil
1 carrot, chopped
1 onion, chopped
1 stalk celery, chopped
1 clove garlic, crushed
440 g/14 oz canned tomatoes,
undrained and mashed
6 cups/1.5 litres/2$^{1}/_{2}$ pt fish stock
440 g/14 oz canned cannellini beans,
rinsed and drained
220 g/7 oz short pasta, such as elbow
macaroni or penne
185 g/6 oz green beans, chopped
250 g/8 oz firm white fish
fillets, cubed
155 g/5 oz mixed seafood such as
mussels, scallops and prawns
1 tablespoon fresh lemon thyme leaves

1 Heat oil in a saucepan over a medium heat, add carrot, onion, celery and garlic and cook for 5 minutes or until vegetables are soft.

2 Add tomatoes and stock to pan, bring to simmering and simmer for 10 minutes. Stir in cannellini beans, pasta and green beans, bring back to simmering and simmer for 12 minutes or until pasta is tender.

3 Add fish, mixed seafood and thyme and cook, stirring occasionally, for 2-4 minutes or until seafood is cooked.

Serves 4

If lemon thyme is unavailable use ordinary thyme and $^{1}/_{2}$ teaspoon finely grated lemon rind.

CHICKEN AND COUSCOUS SALAD

1076 kilojoules/256 Calories per serve – high fibre; low fat; 2 serves carbohydrate

1 cup/185 g/6 oz couscous
$^1/_2$ cup/125 mL/4 fl oz boiling water
$^1/_2$ cup/125 mL/4 fl oz boiling
chicken stock
1 cos lettuce, leaves separated
250 g/8 oz cooked chicken breast
fillets, cut into thick slices
2 tomatoes, chopped
1 cucumber, chopped
3 tablespoons fresh coriander leaves
60 g/2 oz snow pea (mangetout)
sprouts or watercress

YOGURT DRESSING
2 tablespoons chopped fresh mint
1 teaspoon ground cumin
$^1/_2$ teaspoon chilli powder
1 cup/200 g/6$^1/_2$ oz low-fat yogurt

1 Place couscous in a bowl, pour over boiling water and stock, cover and stand for 5 minutes or until water is absorbed. Toss with a fork to separate grains.

2 Arrange lettuce, couscous, chicken, tomatoes, cucumber, coriander and snow pea (mangetout) sprouts or watercress on a serving platter.

3 To make dressing, place mint, cumin, chilli powder and yogurt in a bowl and whisk to combine. Drizzle a little dressing over salad and serve remaining dressing separately.

Serves 4

**EASY CHICKEN
SALAD MEAL**
**Chicken and Couscous
Salad
Warm Flatbread*

*Left: Seafood Minestrone
Above: Chicken and Couscous
Salad*

Meals in a Bowl

Soup packed with vegetables and noodles, legumes, pasta or rice can be a healthy and satisfying meal for anyone. Many soups can be made in advance and stored for a day or two in the refrigerator or frozen to have on hand for a quick meal. Leftovers are an easy lunch and crusty bread of your choice is a great accompaniment.

Dried chickpeas can be used for this recipe but you will need to soak and cook them first.

CHICKPEA AND SPINACH SOUP

830 kilojoules/198 Calories per serve – high fibre; low fat; 1.5 serves carbohydrate

^{1}/2 onion, chopped
^{1}/2 carrot, chopped
1 stalk celery, chopped
2 cloves garlic, crushed
1 teaspoon olive oil
440 g/14 oz canned chickpeas,
rinsed and drained
2 sprigs fresh rosemary
6 cups/1.5 litres/2^1/2 pt vegetable stock
2 x 440 g/14 oz canned tomatoes,
undrained and mashed
1 bunch/500 g/1 lb English spinach,
stalks removed

1 Place onion, carrot, celery and garlic into a food processor and process to make a purée.

2 Place vegetable mixture and oil in a saucepan over a medium heat and cook for 5 minutes. Add chickpeas, rosemary, stock and tomatoes and bring to the boil. Reduce heat and simmer for 30 minutes. Add spinach and serve immediately.

Serves 4

Oven temperature
220°C, 425°F, Gas 7

BASIL SCONES

643 kilojoules/153 Calories per scone – low fibre; low fat; 1.5 serves carbohydrate

2 cups/250 g/8 oz self-raising flour
15 g/^{1}/2 oz butter
4 tablespoons shredded basil
2 teaspoons cracked black pepper
1 cup/250 mL/8 fl oz milk

1 Place flour and butter in a food processor and process until mixture resembles coarse breadcrumbs.

2 With machine running, add basil, black pepper and milk and process until a smooth dough forms. Place dough on a lightly floured surface and using the palm of your hand, press out to 3 cm/ 1^1/4 in thick, then using a 5 cm/2 in cutter, cut out rounds. Place scones in a nonstick 20 cm/8 in round cake tin and bake for 15 minutes or until golden.

Makes 8

Other fresh herbs such as parsley or coriander could be used in these scones instead of the basil.

Previous pages: Chickpea and Spinach Soup, Basil Scones
Opposite: Vietnamese Chicken Broth

VIETNAMESE CHICKEN BROTH

2022 kilojoules/481 Calories per serve – low fibre; low fat; 5 serves carbohydrate

5 cm/2 in piece knob ginger, sliced
1 tablespoon black peppercorns
2 star anise
6 cups/1.5 litres/2¹/₂ pt chicken stock
2 boneless chicken breast fillets
375 g/12 oz fresh rice noodles
90 g/3 oz bean sprouts
2 shallots, sliced
2 tablespoons Vietnamese mint leaves

1   Place ginger, peppercorns and star anise in a piece of muslin and tie with string to make a bag.

2   Place stock and spice bag in a saucepan over a medium heat, bring to the boil, then reduce heat and simmer for 10 minutes. Add chicken and cook for 6-8 minutes or until tender. Remove chicken from stock, cut into thin slices and set aside. Discard spice bag.

3   Place noodles in a bowl, pour over boiling water to cover and stand for 3 minutes or until soft. Drain.

4   To serve, divide noodles between deep serving bowls. Top with bean sprouts, chicken, shallots and mint, ladle over stock and serve immediately.

Serving Suggestion: Serve soup with small bowls of chopped fresh red chillies, hoisin and fish sauces and lime wedges. Each diner then adds seasonings to taste.

Serves 4

VIETNAMESE SOUP MEAL
**Vietnamese Chicken Broth
Rockmelon (cantaloupe) topped with Fresh Passion Fruit Pulp*

If Vietnamese mint is unavailable, ordinary mint or basil are good alternatives. Fresh rice noodles are made from a paste of ground rice and water which is then cut into strips. They are very delicate and require only the briefest of cooking or soaking in boiling water. They are available in a variety of widths from Oriental food shops and some supermarkets.

WINTER SOUP MEAL
*Leek and Ham Soup
*Potato Croûtons
*Baked Bananas in
Orange Juice
(see hint this page)*

LEEK AND HAM SOUP

823 kilojoules/196 Calories per serve – high fibre; low fat; 1.5 serves carbohydrate

2 teaspoons vegetable oil
2 leeks, chopped
185g/6 oz green split peas
4 slices reduced-salt and -fat ham,
chopped
2 bay leaves
3 cups/750 mL/1¼ pt beef stock
3 cups/750 mL/1¼ pt water
2 tablespoons chopped fresh parsley
freshly ground black pepper

1   Heat oil in a saucepan over a medium heat, add leeks and cook, stirring, for 7 minutes or until soft and golden.

2   Add peas, ham, bay leaves, stock and water, bring to boil, then reduce heat and simmer for 45-60 minutes or until peas dissolve into soup. Stir in parsley and black pepper to taste. Serve topped with Potato Croûtons (see recipe below).

Serves 4

POTATO CROUTONS

170 kilojoules/40 Calories per serve – medium fibre; low fat; 2 serves carbohydrate

Oven temperature
180°C, 350°F, Gas 4

2 potatoes, diced
vegetable oil spray

Place potatoes on a baking tray lined with nonstick baking paper. Spray potatoes with oil and bake for 30 minutes or until crisp and golden.

Serves 4

7 WAYS TO REDUCE FAT

For an easy hot dessert try Baked Bananas in Orange Juice. To make, peel and cut 4 bananas into thick slices. Place bananas in an ovenproof dish, pour over the juice of 1 fresh orange, drizzle with a little honey and sprinkle with ground cinnamon to taste. Cover and bake at 180°C/350°F/ Gas 4 for 10-15 minutes or until bananas are tender.

*Potato Croûtons,
Leek and Ham Soup*

One of the easiest ways to reduce the amount of fat you eat is to use less fat when you cook.

1   Avoid frying in oil, butter, margarine or ghee. Try grilling, roasting on a rack, steaming or microwave cooking instead.

2   Always trim all visible fat from meat. Remove fat and skin from chicken. Look for lean cuts of meat and limit the amount of sausages, luncheon meats and salamis you eat.

3   Use a nonstick frying pan and simply brush or spray with a little oil (don't pour oil in) for browning and sautéeing.

4   Change the emphasis of your meals. Eat more pasta, rice, vegetables, bread and fruit, and less meat and fatty sauces.

5   Cook casseroles and soups one day ahead and chill. Any fat will rise to the surface and can be easily removed once it solidifies.

6   Use low-fat or skim milk in cooking whenever possible. Choose cottage or ricotta cheese in place of cream cheese and sour cream.

7   Try low-fat, unflavoured yogurt in place of sour cream to finish casseroles. Do not reboil or the yogurt will curdle.

Something to Celebrate

Entertaining family and friends is one of the great pleasures in life, however more often than not slimmers are faced with the problem of food that does not fit into a healthy eating plan. Here you will find two menus that are special enough to serve for a celebration, but healthy enough that you too can enjoy them.

If green (unripe) mangoes
are unavailable, use very
tart green apples instead.
Ripe mangoes will give the
salad a different flavour
and texture.

Oven temperature
160°C, 325°F, Gas 3

To cook white rice in the
microwave, place 1 cup/
220 g/7 oz rice and 2 cups/
500 mL/16 fl oz water in a
microwavable container.
Cook, uncovered on HIGH
(100%) for 12-15 minutes or
until liquid is absorbed. Cover
and stand for 5 minutes, then
toss with a fork. If cooking
brown rice, add an extra
1 cup/250 mL/8 fl oz of water
and increase the cooking
time to 30-35 minutes.

*Previous pages: Lime Leaf
Stir-fried Greens, Chicken in Paper
Right: Grilled Prawn Salad*

GRILLED PRAWN SALAD

702 kilojoules/167 Calories per serve – medium fibre; low fat; 1.5 serves carbohydrate

16 uncooked prawns, shelled and
deveined, tails left intact
1 fresh green chilli, seeded and shredded
1/4 cup/60 mL/2 fl oz reduced-salt
soy sauce
1 tablespoon honey
1 witlof (chicory), leaves separated
1 radicchio, leaves separated
2 green (unripe) mangoes, thinly sliced
4 tablespoons fresh mint leaves
3 tablespoons fresh coriander leaves
1 tablespoon brown sugar
2 tablespoons lime juice

1 Place prawns, chilli, soy sauce and
honey in a bowl, toss to combine and
marinate for 5 minutes.

2 Arrange witlof (chicory), radicchio,
mangoes, mint and coriander on serving
plates. Combine sugar and lime juice
and drizzle over salad.

3 Heat a nonstick frying pan over a
high heat, add prawns and stir-fry for
2 minutes or until cooked. Place prawns
on top of salad, spoon over pan juices
and serve immediately.

Serves 4

CHICKEN IN PAPER

780 kilojoules/186 Calories per serve – high fibre; low fat; 0.3 serve carbohydrate

1 bulb fennel, sliced
4 plum (egg or Italian) tomatoes,
quartered
4 small boneless chicken breast fillets,
skin removed
125 g/4 oz oyster mushrooms
1 tablespoon wholegrain mustard
1/4 cup/60 mL/2 fl oz white wine

1 Cut four rectangles of nonstick
baking paper large enough to completely
enclose vegetables and chicken. The
paper should be at least 10 cm/4 in
larger than fillets on all sides. Place
some fennel slices, a tomato, a chicken
breast fillet and some oyster mushrooms
slightly to one side of the centre of each
piece of paper.

2 Place mustard and wine in a small
bowl and whisk to combine. Drizzle
mustard mixture over chicken, then fold
paper over so the long sides meet and
fold edges to seal. Fold over ends to
make a parcel. Place parcels on a baking
tray and bake for 20 minutes or until
chicken is tender.

Serves 4

LIME LEAF STIR-FRIED GREENS

289 kilojoules/69 Calories per serve – medium fibre; low fat; 0.6 serve carbohydrate

1 teaspoon sesame oil
3 spring onions, chopped
1 tablespoon shredded fresh ginger
4 kaffir lime leaves, shredded
2 teaspoons brown sugar
1/4 cup/60 mL/2 fl oz oyster sauce
250 g/8 oz bok choy (Chinese leaves), chopped
155 g/5 oz snake (yard-long) or green beans, chopped
155 g/5 oz sugar snap peas

1   Heat sesame oil in a nonstick frying pan over a high heat, add spring onions and ginger and stir-fry for 1 minute. Stir in lime leaves, sugar and oyster sauce and stir-fry for 2 minutes.

2   Add bok choy (Chinese leaves), beans and peas to pan and stir-fry for 3-4 minutes or until vegetables are bright green and tender crisp.

Serves 4

Kaffir lime leaves are the leaves of the kaffir lime tree, a citrus tree native to South-East Asia. They are available fresh or fresh frozen from Oriental food shops and some greengrocers. If unavailable, a little finely shredded lime rind can be used instead. For this recipe use fresh or fresh frozen leaves not dried.

Above: Grilled Sugared Pears
Right: Apple and Blueberry Crumble

GRILLED SUGARED PEARS

405 kilojoules/96 Calories per serve – medium fibre; low fat; 1.5 serves carbohydrate

2 pears, peeled, halved and cored
1 teaspoon vanilla essence
3 tablespoons brown sugar

1 Place pears in a shallow ovenproof dish. Brush with vanilla essence and sprinkle with sugar.

2 Place under a preheated hot grill and cook for 2-3 minutes or until golden.

Serving suggestion: Place pears on warm serving plates, spoon over any cooking juices and accompany with low-fat yogurt ice cream.

Serves 4

Other fruits such as peaches, apples, nectarines and plums are also delicious cooked in this way.

APPLE AND BLUEBERRY CRUMBLE

1656 kilojoules/394 Calories per serve – high fibre; medium fat; 5 serves carbohydrate

4 apples, cored and chopped
375 g/12 oz fresh or frozen blueberries
2 teaspoons finely grated lemon rind
1 teaspoon ground cinnamon

CRUMBLE TOPPING
1¹/₂ cups/140 g/4¹/₂ oz rolled oats
¹/₂ cup/90 g/3 oz brown sugar
30 g/1 oz butter, softened
¹/₂ cup/125 mL/4 fl oz orange juice

1 Place apples, blueberries, lemon rind and cinnamon in an ovenproof dish and toss to combine.

2 To make topping, place rolled oats, sugar, butter and orange juice in a food processor and process briefly to combine. Sprinkle topping over fruit and bake for 35 minutes or until top is golden and fruit is soft.

Serving suggestion: Accompany with low-fat honey yogurt.

Serves 4

CASUAL WINTER
DINNER PARTY
*Spicy Lamb Skewers
*Minted Tomato Couscous
*Stir-fried Sweet Peppers
*Apple and Blueberry
Crumble
Low-fat Honey-flavoured
Yogurt

Oven temperature
180°C, 350°F, Gas 4

SPICY LAMB SKEWERS

732 kilojoules/174 Calories per serve – low fibre; medium fat; negligible carbohydrate

**500 g/1 lb lamb fillet, trimmed of
visible fat and cut into thin strips**

COCONUT AND CORIANDER
MARINADE
**2 tablespoons chopped fresh coriander
1 tablespoon red curry paste
$^1/_3$ cup/90 mL/3 fl oz reduced-fat
coconut milk**

1   Thread lamb strips onto lightly
oiled skewers.

2   To make marinade, place coriander,
curry paste and coconut milk in a bowl
and mix to combine. Brush marinade
over lamb and marinate for 20 minutes.

3   Heat a nonstick char-grill pan over a
high heat, add lamb skewers and cook
for 1-2 minutes each side or until tender.

Serves 4

These skewers can also be
cooked on the barbecue or
under a preheated grill.

MINTED TOMATO COUSCOUS

771 kilojoules/184 Calories per serve – medium fibre; low fat; 2.5 serves carbohydrate

**$1^1/_2$ cups/280 g/9 oz couscous
$1^1/_2$ cups/375 mL/12 fl oz hot
chicken stock
3 tablespoons sun-dried tomatoes,
without oil
2 tablespoons chopped fresh mint
4 spring onions, chopped**

1   Place couscous in a heatproof bowl,
pour over stock, cover and stand for
10 minutes or until liquid is absorbed.

2   Place a nonstick frying pan over a
low heat, add couscous, tomatoes, mint
and spring onions and cook, stirring, for
7 minutes or until heated through.

Serves 4

This easy dish is a great
low-fat accompaniment to
casseroles and stews. Try it
instead of mashed potatoes
as a side dish to the Lamb
with Quinces on page 41.

STIR-FRIED SWEET PEPPERS

282 kilojoules/67 Calories per serve – medium fibre; low fat; 0.5 serve carbohydrate

**1 teaspoon sesame oil
1 red pepper, cut into thin strips
1 yellow pepper, cut into thin strips
1 green pepper, cut into thin strips
3 tablespoons hoisin sauce
2 teaspoons sesame seeds**

1   Heat oil in a nonstick wok or frying
pan over a medium heat, add peppers and
stir-fry for 2-3 minutes or until tender.

2   Stir in hoisin sauce and cook for
1-2 minutes longer. Scatter with sesame
seeds and serve.

Serves 4

*Stir-fried Sweet Peppers, Spicy
Lamb Skewers on Minted Tomato
Couscous*

Time for a Snack

Well planned snacks can be part of a healthy eating plan and will often save the slimmer from overeating at other times. Fresh fruit and vegetables, breads and low-fat yogurt are all great snack foods, however there are times when you want something a little more indulgent – the recipes in this chapter may well be the answer!

OAT AND BANANA COOKIES

387 kilojoules/92 Calories per cookie – low fibre; low fat; 1 serve carbohydrate

Oven temperature
180°C, 350°F, Gas 4

1^1/2 cups/140 g/4^1/2 oz rolled oats
^{1}/2 cup/60 g/2 oz flour
1 teaspoon bicarbonate of soda
^{2}/3 cup/100 g/3^1/2 oz brown sugar
1 teaspoon ground cinnamon
2 ripe bananas, mashed
60 g/2 oz butter or margarine, melted
1 teaspoon vanilla essence

When freshly cooked these cookies will be quite soft but as they cool they harden.

1 Place oats, flour and bicarbonate of soda in a bowl and mix to combine.

2 Place sugar, cinnamon, bananas, butter or margarine and vanilla essence in a bowl and mix to combine. Add banana mixture to dry ingredients and mix to combine.

3 Drop tablespoons of mixture onto baking paper-lined or nonstick baking trays and bake for 10 minutes or until golden. Stand cookies on trays for 2-3 minutes then carefully transfer to wire racks to cool.

Makes 20

BROWNIE CUPCAKES

470 kilojoules/112 Calories per cake – low fibre; low fat; 1 serve carbohydrate

Oven temperature
180°C, 350°F, Gas 4

^{3}/4 cup/90 g/3 oz flour
^{1}/2 cup/45 g/1^1/2 oz cocoa powder
^{1}/2 teaspoon baking powder
1 cup/220 g/7 oz caster sugar
^{1}/2 cup/100 g/3^1/2 oz low-fat vanilla yogurt
2 eggs
1^1/2 tablespoons vegetable oil
1 teaspoon vanilla essence

For an easy low-fat treat or dessert serve these cakes warm with fresh fruit and low-fat natural yogurt.

1 Sift flour and cocoa and baking powders together in a bowl. Add sugar, yogurt, eggs, oil and vanilla essence and mix well.

2 Spoon mixture into patty pans (tins) lined with patty cases and bake for 15 minutes or until cakes are firm.

Makes 16

RASPBERRY AND LIME MUFFINS

727 kilojoules/173 Calories per muffin – low fibre; low fat; 2 serves carbohydrate

Oven temperature
190°C, 375°F, Gas 5

2 cups/250 g/8 oz self-raising flour
^{1}/2 cup/90 g/3 oz brown sugar
2 ripe bananas, mashed
2 teaspoons finely grated lime rind
1 cup/200 g/6^1/2 oz vanilla-flavoured yogurt
^{1}/2 cup/125 mL/4 fl oz milk or buttermilk
1 egg, lightly beaten
30 g/1 oz butter or margarine, melted
1 cup fresh or frozen raspberries

*Previous pages; Brownie Cupcakes, Raspberry and Lime Muffins, Oat and Banana Cookies
Right: Sugar-grilled Banana Bagels*

1 Place flour and sugar in a bowl and mix to combine. Add bananas, lime rind, yogurt, milk, egg and butter or margarine and mix until just combined. Fold raspberries into batter.

2 Spoon batter into twelve ^{1}/2 cup/125 mL/4 fl oz capacity muffin tins and bake for 25-30 minutes or until cooked when tested with a skewer.

Makes 12

SUGAR-GRILLED BANANA BAGELS

971 kilojoules/231 Calories per half bagel – low fibre; low fat; 3 serves carbohydrate

2 fruit or plain bagels, split
$^1/_2$ cup/125 g/4 oz low-fat ricotta
cheese, drained
$^1/_2$ teaspoon ground cinnamon
2 tablespoons maple syrup
2 bananas, sliced
brown sugar

1　Place bagels, cut side down under a preheated hot grill and lightly toast.

2　Place ricotta cheese, cinnamon and maple syrup in a food processor or blender and process to combine. Spread ricotta mixture over untoasted side of bagels, then top with bananas and sprinkle with sugar. Place under grill and cook for 1-2 minutes or until bananas are golden.

Serves 2-4

Bananas are a great instant snack or dessert for slimmers and the health-conscious. When eaten raw, they require no preparation, taste great, are high in fibre, low in fat and protein and are rich in minerals (especially potassium and magnesium).

EGGPLANT AND GARLIC DIP

136 kilojoules/32 Calories per 2 tablespoons – medium fibre; low fat; 0.3 serve carbohydrate

Oven temperature
220°C, 425°F, Gas 7

For a smoky flavour cook the eggplant (aubergines) on a preheated barbecue grill until skins are charred and flesh is soft.

2 eggplant (aubergines)
2 tablespoons chopped fresh mint
2 cloves garlic, crushed
1 teaspoon ground cumin
$^3/_4$ cup/155 g/5 oz low-fat
natural yogurt
$^1/_4$ cup/60 mL/2 fl oz lemon juice
freshly ground black pepper

1 Place eggplant (aubergines) in a baking dish and bake for 25 minutes or until skins are charred and eggplant (aubergines) are very soft. Set aside until cool enough to handle, then remove skins.

2 Place eggplant (aubergine) flesh, mint, garlic, cumin, yogurt, lemon juice and black pepper to taste in a food processor and process until smooth.

Serving suggestion: Serve with toasted flatbread or baked pitta bread.

Serves 4

CRISPY POTATO WEDGES

1046 kilojoules/249 Calories per serve – high fibre; low fat; 3 serves carbohydrate

Oven temperature
200°C, 400°F, Gas 6

These healthy potato wedges make a great snack or are delicious as a side dish to a main meal.
Not only do these potato wedges taste delicious, but they have the added benefit of being lower in fat and salt than the commercially prepared varieties.

4 large potatoes, scrubbed
vegetable oil spray
sweet chilli sauce for dipping

CORIANDER YOGURT DIP
$^1/_4$ cup/45 g/1$^1/_2$ oz low-fat
natural yogurt
1 tablespoon chopped fresh coriander
freshly ground black pepper

1 Cook potatoes in boiling water for 6 minutes. Drain and cut into wedges.

2 Place wedges on a baking tray lined with nonstick baking paper, spray lightly with oil and bake for 15-20 minutes or until wedges are crisp and golden.

3 To make dip, place yogurt, coriander and black pepper to taste in a bowl and mix to combine. Serve wedges with dip and sweet chilli sauce.

Serves 2-3

*Eggplant and Garlic Dip,
Crispy Potato Wedges*

Wickedly Good Desserts

For many a meal without a dessert is incomplete, however it can be the downfall for many slimmers. The selection of desserts in this chapter look a lot more indulgent than they are – remember, stick to the suggested serving size and there will no problems with including them as part of your weight loss plan.

CHOCOLATE FUDGE CAKE

767 kilojoules/183 Calories per serve – low fibre; low fat; 2 serves carbohydrate

Oven temperature
160°C, 325°F, Gas 3

²/₃ cup/60 g/2 oz cocoa powder
²/₃ cup/170 mL/5¹/₂ fl oz boiling water
4 egg yolks
1 cup/250 g/8 oz sugar
³/₄ cup/90 g/3 oz flour, sifted
6 egg whites

Store high temptation food in containers, in cupboards or at the back of the refrigerator. Better still don't buy foods such as confectionery and high-fat snack foods which you know will be hard to resist.

1 Place cocoa powder in a bowl, add water and stir until dissolved.

2 Place egg yolks and ¹/₂ cup/125 g/4 oz sugar in a bowl and beat for 5 minutes or until mixture is until thick and creamy. Fold cocoa mixture and flour, alternately, into egg yolk mixture.

3 Place egg whites in a clean bowl and beat until soft peaks form. Gradually beat in remaining sugar and continue beating until thick and glossy.

4 Fold egg whites into egg yolk mixture. Pour mixture into a 23 cm/9 in springform tin, base lined with nonstick baking paper and bake for 25 minutes or until cake is just firm to touch.

Serving suggestion: Cut cake into wedges and serve with raspberry couli. To make couli, place 250 g/8 oz fresh or thawed frozen raspberries in a food processor or blender and purée. Press purée through a sieve to remove seeds.

Serves 8

PANNA COTTA WITH RHUBARB

825 kilojoules/196 Calories per serve – medium fibre; medium fat; 1.5 serves carbohydrate

¹/₄ cup/60 mL/2 fl oz water
3 teaspoons gelatine
¹/₂ cup/125 g/4 oz sugar
¹/₃ cup/90 mL/3 fl oz cream
2¹/₂ cups/600 mL/1 pt buttermilk
2 teaspoons vanilla essence

SIMMERED RHUBARB AND LIME
5 stalks rhubarb, chopped
4 strips lime rind
¹/₂ cup/125 mL/4 fl oz orange juice
sugar to taste

Rinsing the ramekins with cold water before filling with the Panna Cotta mixture makes it easier to turn them out once set.

1 Place water in a saucepan over a medium heat and bring to simmering. Sprinkle gelatine over water and stir to dissolve.

2 Stir in sugar and cream and heat until almost boiling. Remove pan from heat and whisk in buttermilk and vanilla essence. Pour mixture into six ³/₄ cup/185 mL/6 fl oz capacity ramekins and refrigerate until set.

3 For rhubarb, place rhubarb, lime rind and orange juice in a saucepan over a medium heat, cover and cook for 6 minutes or until rhubarb is tender. Add sugar to taste and remove lime rind.

4 Serve Panna Cotta in ramekins or turn onto serving plates and accompany with rhubarb.

Serves 6

Previous pages; Panna Cotta with Rhubarb, Chocolate Fudge Cake Right: Lemon Cheesecake

LEMON CHEESECAKE

573 kilojoules/136 Calories per serve – low fibre; low fat; 1 serve carbohydrate

2 cups/500 g/1 lb low-fat cottage
cheese, drained
1 cup/250 g/8 oz low-fat ricotta
cheese, drained
$^1/_3$ cup/90 g/3 oz sugar
1 cup/200 g/6$^1/_2$ oz thick natural yogurt
2 eggs
$^1/_4$ cup/30 g/1 oz cornflour
1 tablespoon finely grated lemon rind

1   Place cottage and ricotta cheeses,
sugar, yogurt and eggs in a food processor
and process until smooth. Add cornflour
and lemon rind and process to combine.

2   Pour mixture into a lightly greased
23 cm/9 in round cake tin and place
in a baking dish with enough water to
come halfway up the sides of the tin.
Bake for 45 minutes or until cake is firm
to touch. Cool cheesecake in tin.

Serving suggestion: Cut cheesecake
into wedges and accompany with fresh
seasonal fruit.

Serves 10

Oven temperature
150°C, 300°F, Gas 2

For a lime or orange version
of this delicious dessert,
replace the lemon rind with
lime or orange rind.

PEACH CRISP

881 kilojoules/210 Calories per serve – low fibre; low fat; 2.5 serves carbohydrate

Oven temperature
180°C, 350°F, Gas 4

Eating slowly allows more time for your stomach to signal your brain that you are full. So take smaller bites; chew each mouthful well; put your knife and fork down between bites and aim to be the last to finish not the first.

vegetable oil spray
3 sheets filo pastry
2 tablespoons sugar
1/2 cup/125 g/4 oz low-fat ricotta cheese, drained
1/2 cup/100 g/3 1/2 oz low-fat honey-flavoured yogurt
1 tablespoon lemon juice
3-4 fresh peaches, sliced or 6-8 canned peach halves in natural juice, drained
1/4 cup/60 g/2 oz demerara or raw sugar

1 Spray each sheet of pastry lightly with oil, then layer and cut into eight rectangles. Place on a baking tray lined with nonstick baking paper. Sprinkle with sugar and bake for 7-8 minutes or until pastry is crisp and golden.

2 Place ricotta cheese, yogurt and lemon juice in a food processor or blender and process until smooth. Spread a little of the ricotta mixture over each pastry rectangle, then top with peach slices and sprinkle with demerara or raw sugar. Place under a preheated hot grill and cook for 1 minute or until sugar melts. To serve, make a stack using two pastries. Serve immediately.

Serves 4

BANANA BREAD PUDDING

2092 kilojoules/498 Calories per serve – high fibre; medium fat; 6 serves carbohydrate

8 slices fruit bread, crusts trimmed
3 bananas, sliced
¹/4 cup/60 g/2 oz sugar, plus
2 tablespoons extra
1 teaspoon ground cinnamon
2¹/2 cups/600 mL/1 pt reduced-fat milk
3 eggs

1 Place alternate layers of bread and bananas in four 1¹/4 cup/315 mL/10 fl oz capacity ramekins. Set aside.

2 Place ¹/4 cup/60 g/2 oz sugar, cinnamon, milk and eggs in a bowl and whisk to combine. Pour over bread and bananas in ramekins and place in a baking dish with enough water to come halfway up the sides of the ramekins. Sprinkle tops of puddings with extra sugar and bake for 20-25 minutes or until puddings are firm.

Serves 4

Oven temperature
160°C, 325°F, Gas 3

Above: Banana Bread Pudding
Left: Peach Crisp

14-Day Meal Planner

NUTRITIONAL ANALYSIS
The daily nutritional analysis is based on the following requirements and ensures a balanced eating plan for weight loss:

Kilojoules	5000-6000
Calories	1190-1429
Fat	20 g
Protein	100-200 g
Carbohydrate	
women	120-150 g
men	150-180 g
Fibre	25-35 g

DAILY ALLOWANCE
Each day you have an allowance for milk and fats as follows:

Milk: 315 mL/10 fl oz low-fat (light/lite) milk or 450 mL/ 15 fl oz skim milk for use in tea, coffee, milk drinks, on cereal and in cooking.

Fats: 1 tablespoon oil (any type), plus 1 tablespoon margarine or butter (or 2 tablespoons reduced-fat spread) for spreading and cooking.

DAY 1
5357 kilojoules/1275 Calories
19 g fat; 77 g protein; 194 g carbohydrate; 25 g fibre

BREAKFAST
1 wedge rockmelon (cantaloupe)

$1/2$ cup/100 g/$3^1/2$ oz low-fat natural yogurt

1 tablespoon unprocessed wheat bran

LUNCH
Salad made with 100 g/$3^1/2$ oz drained, tuna in brine or springwater, thin slices cucumber, lettuce, $1/2$ red pepper, capers and 1 tablespoon no-oil dressing

1 Raspberry and Lime Muffin (page 68)

DINNER
Marinated Tomato Salad (page 24)

Penne with Pepper Sauce (page 24)

Tossed Green Salad with Lemon (page 42)

Apple and Ricotta Strudel (page 25)

DAY 2
4963 kiljoules/1182 Calories
22 g fat; 81 g protein; 163 g carbohydrate; 27 g fibre

BREAKFAST
1 orange, cut into segments

1 boiled or poached egg

1 slice wholemeal bread, toasted and lightly spread with margarine or reduced-fat spread from allowance

LUNCH
1 crusty wholemeal roll filled with 30 g/1 oz cold chicken (skin removed), lettuce, cucumber and grated carrot

1 piece fresh fruit

DINNER
Lime Marinated Fish (page 48)

Sweet Potato Mash (page 48)

Steamed Greens with Lime (page 48)

1 cup/200 g/$6^1/2$ oz low-fat fruit yogurt

DAY 3
5151 kilojoules/1226 Calories
22 g fat; 79 g protein; 186 g carbohydrate; 32 g fibre

BREAKFAST
$3/4$ cup/30 g/1 oz breakfast cereal (flakes), sprinkled with 2 tablespoons oat or barley bran, topped with low-fat or skim milk from allowance

1 banana

LUNCH
1 wholemeal pitta bread, split and filled with 30 g/1 oz cold lamb or beef, shredded lettuce, tabbouleh and beetroot

Fresh fruit salad topped with low-fat yogurt and poppy seeds

DINNER
Beef Tortillas with Salsa (page 35)

1 piece fresh fruit

DAY 4
5289 kilojoules/1259 Calories
13 g fat; 87 g protein; 195 g carbohydrate; 24 g fibre

BREAKFAST
$1/2$ grapefruit

1 slice mulitgrain bread, toasted and topped with 30 g/1 oz low-fat cottage cheese and tomato slices

Berry milkshake made with fresh berries of your choice, skim or low-fat milk from allowance and honey

LUNCH
1 mug clear vegetable soup

1 baked jacket potato, topped with low-fat cottage cheese and 1 slice (20 g/$3/4$ oz) chopped reduced-salt and -fat ham and snipped fresh chives

Tossed salad of assorted lettuce leaves

1 cup/200 g/$6^1/2$ oz low-fat fruit yogurt

DINNER
Chicken and Couscous Salad (page 51)

Warm flatbread

Low-fat ice cream and fresh fruit

DAY 5

4751 kilojoules/1131 Calories
22 g fat; 72 g protein; 144 g carbohydrate; 24 g fibre

BREAKFAST

1 wedge rockmelon (cantaloupe)

1 bran muffin, topped with 20 g/^{3}/4 oz reduced-fat Cheddar cheese, grilled

LUNCH

1 crusty wholemeal roll moistened with a little no-fat mayonnaise and filled with 45 g/1^1/2 oz canned salmon in springwater and coleslaw

1 piece fresh fruit

DINNER

Stuffed Peppers (page 44)

Baked Sicilian Fish (page 44)

Warm Potato Salad (page 20)

DAY 6

4671 kilojoules/1112 Calories
16 g fat; 63 g protein; 178 g carbohydrate; 32 g fibre

BREAKFAST

^{1}/2 grapefruit

1 Weet Bix (Weetabix) sprinkled with 2 teaspoons oat or barley bran, topped with low-fat or skim milk from allowance

1 slice multigrain bread, toasted and lightly spread with margarine or reduced-fat spread from allowance

LUNCH

1 mug clear vegetable soup

^{1}/2 cup/125 g/4 oz canned reduced-salt baked beans served on a slice of wholemeal toast (no spread needed)

DINNER

Leek and Ham Soup (page 56)

Potato Croûtons (page 56)

Baked Bananas in Orange Juice (page 56)

DAY 7

5116 kilojoules/1218 Calories
16 g fat; 90 g protein; 176 g carbohydrate; 24 g fibre

BREAKFAST

1 wedge honeydew or rockmelon (cantaloupe)

^{1}/2 cup/60 g/2 oz untoasted muesli topped with low-fat or skim milk from allowance

LUNCH

1 lean beef hamburger (100 g/3^1/2 oz) served on ^{1}/2 toasted wholemeal roll or hamburger bun, topped with tomato, shredded lettuce, beetroot and cucumber

1 pear or apple

DINNER

Honey Sesame Chicken (page 12)

Vegetable Soy Noodles (page 12)

Fresh tropical fruit

DAY 8

4717 kilojoules/1123 Calories
23 g fat; 50 g protein; 176 g carbohydrate; 32 g fibre

BREAKFAST

1 bowl fresh fruit salad

^{1}/2 bran muffin, toasted and lightly spread with peanut butter

LUNCH

1 wholemeal sandwich filled with 60 g/2 oz reduced-salt and -fat ham, lettuce, cucumber, grated carrot and bean sprouts

1 piece fresh fruit

DINNER

Chickpea and Spinach Soup (page 54)

Basil Scones (page 54)

Oat and Banana Cookie (page 68)

DAY 9

5079 kilojoules/1209 Calories
14 g fat; 59 g protein; 197 g carbohydrate; 27 g fibre

BREAKFAST

1 wedge rockmelon (cantaloupe) or pawpaw

1 boiled or poached egg

1 thick slice multigrain bread, toasted spread lightly with margarine or reduced-fat spread from allowance

LUNCH

1 bowl boiled wholemeal pasta with tomato sauce

Tossed green salad with a drizzle of no-oil dressing

2 small kiwifruit or mandarins

DINNER

Thai Squid Salad (page 19)

Soy Rice Noodles (page 19)

Fresh fruit with lemon sorbet

LOW-FAT SNACKS

Choose 2-3 of the following low-fat snacks each day:

- 1 piece of fresh fruit
- ^{1}/2 cup/100 g/3^1/2 oz canned fruit in light syrup
- fresh vegetable sticks such as carrots, celery or red, green or yellow peppers
- tomatoes
- raw or lightly cooked fresh vegetables
- canned vegetables such as asparagus or beetroot
- 3-4 crispbreads (use spread from allowance if necessary)
- 1 slice wholemeal or multigrain bread or toast (use spread from allowance if necessary)
- diet soup
- low-fat cottage cheese
- low-fat fruche
- low-fat ice cream confection
- low-fat or diet yogurt
- see also Free Food list on page 6
- Oat and Banana Cookie (page 68)
- Brownie Cupcake (page 68)
- Raspberry and Lime Muffin (page 68)
- ^{1}/2 Sugar-grilled Banana Bagel (page 69)
- Eggplant and Garlic Dip (page 70) with 1 slice bread of your choice
- Crispy Potato Wedges with Coriander Yogurt Dip (page 70)

Slimmers should choose from the following beverages: tea, coffee, low-fat or skim milk (from allowance), iced water, mineral water, soda water or diet soft drink.

DAY 10

4629 kilojoules/1102 Calories
23 g fat; 69 g protein; 154 g carbohydrate; 28 g fibre

BREAKFAST

1 glass tomato juice

1 slice multigrain bread, toasted and topped with 2 grilled tomato halves and snipped fresh chives

LUNCH

1 wholemeal toasted sandwich filled with 30 g/1 oz reduced-fat Cheddar cheese and tomato slices

1 piece fresh fruit

DINNER

Spicy Lamb and Pasta Bake (page 26)

Spinach Tabbouleh (page 26)

Brownie Cupcake (page 68)

DAY 11

5206 kilojoules/1240 Calories
18 g fat; 101 g protein; 166 g carbohydrate; 24 g fibre

BREAKFAST

$^1/_2$ bowl hot rolled oats sprinkled with 2 tablespoons All-Bran and 2 teaspoons brown sugar and low-fat or skim milk from allowance

1 banana

LUNCH

1 grilled chicken or pork kebab with salad wrapped in a small, wholemeal pitta bread

1 piece fresh fruit

DINNER

Cajun Chicken with Salsa (page 36)

Corn Bread (page 36)

Low-fat ice cream and fresh fruit

DAY 12

5698 kilojoules/1357 Calories
31 g fat; 90 g protein; 180 g carbohydrate; 33 g fibre

BREAKFAST

1 egg, lightly scrambled

1 slice toasted multigrain bread

1 piece fresh fruit

LUNCH

1 mug clear beef broth

1 piece barbecued chicken (skin removed) with small carton (100 g/3$^1/_2$ oz) coleslaw and corn on the cob

1 piece fresh fruit

DINNER

Seafood Minestrone (page 50)

Raspberry and Lime Muffin (page 68)

DAY 13

5327 kilojoules/1268 Calories
17 g fat; 91 g protein; 180 g carbohydrate; 25 g fibre

BREAKFAST

1 Banana Smoothie (page 49)

$^2/_3$ cup/30 g/1 oz bran flakes

$^1/_2$ cup/125 g/4 fl oz low-fat or skim milk from allowance

LUNCH

1 sandwich made with high-fibre bran bread and filled with 30 g/1 oz lean cold lamb or beef, tomato slice and a little tomato relish

1 piece fresh fruit

DINNER

Cucumber and Yogurt Dip (page 40)

Unleavened Bread (page 40)

Lamb with Quinces (page 41)

Beans in Tomato Sauce (page 40)

Mashed potatoes

DAY 14

5059 kilojoules/1205 Calories
13 g fat; 81 g protein; 190 g carbohydrate; 26 g fibre

BREAKFAST

1 wedge honeydew or rockmelon (cantaloupe)

2 wholemeal crumpets, toasted and lightly spread with margarine or reduced-fat spread from allowance (if desired) and topped with $^1/_2$ cup/125 g/4 oz canned reduced-salt baked beans

LUNCH

1 sandwich made with multigrain bread, moistened with a little no-oil mayonnaise and filled with 60 g/2 oz canned tuna in springwater, chopped celery and onion

DINNER

Paella (page 42)

Tossed green salad dressed with sherry vinegar or a no-oil dressing

Orange Salad (page 42)

INDEX